WATERFORD TOWNSHIP
PUBLIC LIBRARY

S0-AAB-279

THE Best OF THE Best

BMX GREATS

BY LORI POLYDOROS

Reading Consultant:
Barbara J. Fox
Reading Specialist
North Carolina State University

CAPSTONE PRESS
a capstone imprint

Blazers is published by Capstone Press,
151 Good Counsel Drive, P.O. Box 669, Mankato, Minnesota 56002.
www.capstonepub.com

Copyright © 2012 by Capstone Press, a Capstone imprint.
All rights reserved.
No part of this publication may be reproduced in whole or in part, or stored in a retrieval system,
or transmitted in any form or by any means, electronic, mechanical, photocopying, recording,
or otherwise, without written permission of the publisher.
For information regarding permission, write to Capstone Press,
151 Good Counsel Drive, P.O. Box 669, Dept. R, Mankato, Minnesota 56002.

Books published by Capstone Press are manufactured with paper
containing at least 10 percent post-consumer waste.

Library of Congress Cataloging-in-Publication Data
Polydoros, Lori, 1968–
    BMX greats / by Lori Polydoros.
        p. cm.—(Blazers, best of the best)
    Includes bibliographical references and index.
    Summary: "Lists and describes the top BMX stars of both the past and present"—Provided
by publisher.
    ISBN 978-1-4296-6501-8 (library binding)
    ISBN 978-1-4296-7243-6 (paperback)
    1. Bicycle motocross—Juvenile literature. I. Title. II. Series.
    GV1049.3.P66 2012
    796.6'2—dc22   2011002460

Editorial Credits
Mandy Robbins, editor; Kyle Grenz, designer; Eric Manske, production specialist

Photo Credits
AP Images: Reed Saxon, 20-21; CORBIS: NewSport/Troy Wayrynen, 12-13, 18-19, 26-27;
Dreamstime: Pkripper50, 1(top), 16-17; Fat Tony, 10-11; Getty Images for T-Mobile, 6-7, Mark
Mainz, 8-9; Getty Images Inc.: Amanda Edwards, cover (top), Feng Li, cover (bottom), Harry
How, 14-15; Jared Souney, 24-25; Shutterstock: Ben Haslam/Haslam Photography, 1 (bottom),
4-5, 28-29; Transworld BMX: Keith Mulligan, 22-23

Artistic Effects
Shutterstock: Ashims, Brandon Bourdages, Pakhnyushcha, sabri deniz kizil

The publisher does not endorse products whose logos may appear on objects in images in this book.

WARNING: Do not attempt to ride a bike or perform BMX stunts without
the appropriate safety gear.

Printed in the United States of America in Stevens Point, Wisconsin.
032011   006111WZF11

TABLE OF CONTENTS

HOURS AND YEARS

BMX greats flip, spin, and twist as they soar through the air. It takes years for riders to make it to the top. These pros practice for hours a day to make crazy stunts look easy.

DENNIS McCOY

(1966-)

Dennis McCoy has been a top BMX rider for more than 25 years. He first pulled a **900** at the X Games in 1995. He did it again in 2010 at the age of 43!

TRICKED OUT!

900
two-and-a-half rotations in the air

FACT Dennis competes in BMX street, flatland, **vert**, and dirt. He is the only rider to ever hold a year-end title in all four events.

vert—a style of BMX riding done in U-shaped ramps called half-pipes

WATERFORD TOWNSHIP
PUBLIC LIBRARY   111641

DAVE MIRRA

(1974-)

Dave Mirra is the BMX rider to beat. He has 27 X Games medals. That's more medals than any other rider. Nineteen of them are gold.

FACT Dave was hit by a drunk driver in 1993. He survived a broken skull and came back to BMX riding as strong as ever.

MAT HOFFMAN

(1972-)

Mat Hoffman is called the "godfather" of **freestyle** BMX. He has invented more than 100 tricks and has won six X Games gold medals.

freestyle–a type of BMX riding that focuses on tricks, stunts, and jumps

FACT   Mat has been the World Vert
Champion 10 times.

MIKE DAY

(1984-)

Mike Day is becoming a top BMX rider. He has won medals in the X Games, BMX World Championships, and the Summer Olympics.

FACT Mike's two brothers, Dave and Matt, are also BMX riders.

JAMIE BESTWICK

(1971-)

FACT Jamie won the 2010 X Games vert gold medal with a double downside tailwhip. He spun the back end of his bike around twice while in midair.

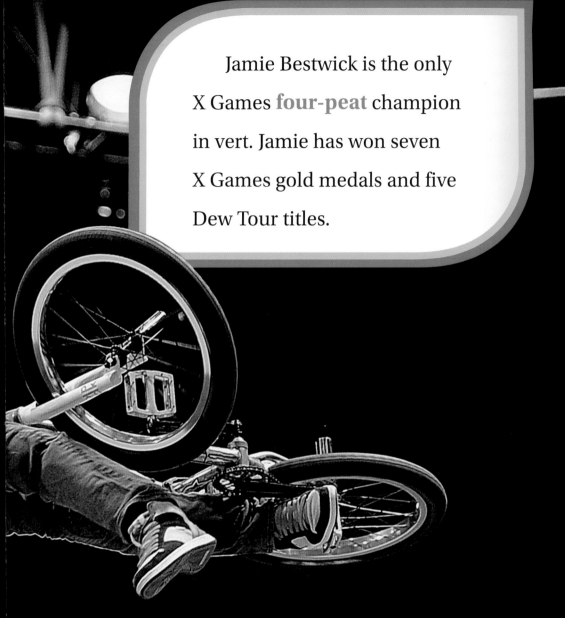

Jamie Bestwick is the only X Games **four-peat** champion in vert. Jamie has won seven X Games gold medals and five Dew Tour titles.

four-peat–describes something done four times in a row

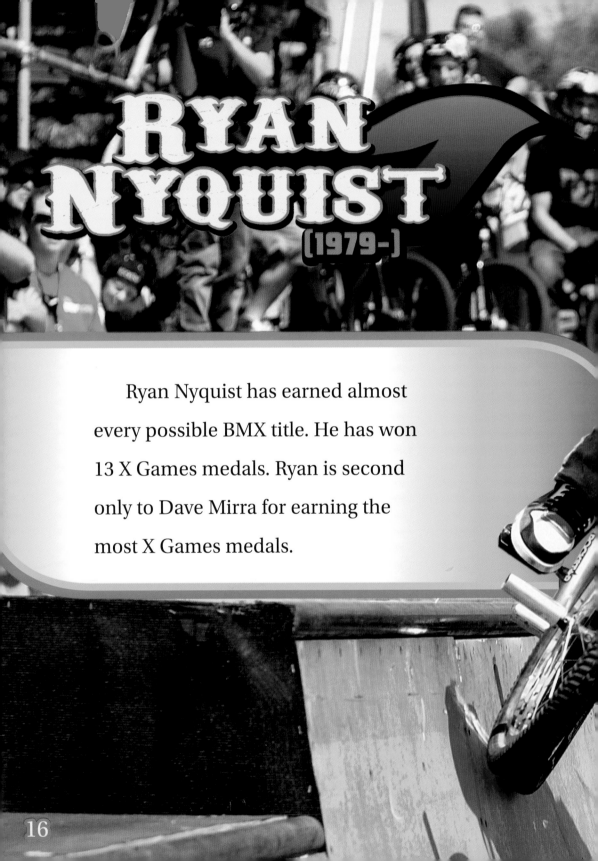

RYAN NYQUIST

(1979-)

Ryan Nyquist has earned almost every possible BMX title. He has won 13 X Games medals. Ryan is second only to Dave Mirra for earning the most X Games medals.

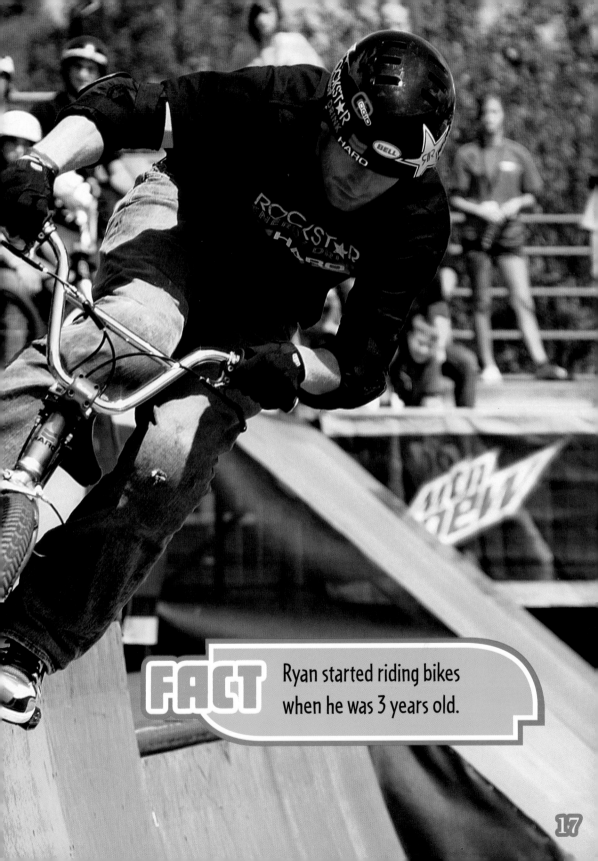

FACT Ryan started riding bikes
when he was 3 years old.

17

Kyle's nickname is "Butter." Fans say he is "smooth like butter" on his bike.

KYLE BENNETT

(1979-)

Kyle Bennett is smooth and quick. He competes on the racetrack and on the X Games downhill courses. In 2008 Kyle raced on the first BMX Olympic team.

MORGAN WADE

(1983-)

Morgan Wade is known for his high-flying style and wild trick combinations. Morgan has performed the highest **quarterpipe airs** on record.

TRICKED OUT!

QUARTERPIPE AIR
a BMX jump done off a quarterpipe; a
quarterpipe looks like one-fourth of a circle

SHAUN BUTLER
(1976-)

Shaun Butler is known for his high-flying dirt jumping style. He was the first rider to do the **superman frame grab**.

TRICKED OUT!

SUPERMAN FRAME GRAB
the rider grabs the bike's frame and stretches his feet out behind him

MIKE DOMINGUEZ

(1968-)

Mike Dominguez is a BMX vert and freestyle **legend**. He invented the no-footed can-can in 1986. Mike was only 12 years old when he turned pro.

FACT Mike started out riding skateboards and then switched to BMX.

legend—someone who is among the best at what they do

Randy "Stumpy" Stumpfhauser has been racing BMX for more than 20 years. He has placed in the top three almost 30 times in major BMX championships.

RANDY STUMPFHAUSER

(1977-)

FACT Randy plans to be a math teacher when he retires from BMX.

TJ ELLIS
(1986-)

TJ Ellis is a rising BMX star. His flip and spin **variations** thrill fans. TJ and other young stars will form the next **generation** of BMX greats.

TJ says his favorite trick is "anything upside down with a backflip!"

variation–a trick that is created by combining other tricks, one after the other

generation–all the members of a group of people born around the same time

GLOSSARY

four-peat (FOR-peet)—describes something done four times in a row

frame (FRAYM)—the body of a bike

freestyle (FREE-styl)—a type of BMX riding that focuses on tricks, stunts, and jumps

generation (jen-uh-RAY-shuhn)—all the members of a group of people born around the same time

legend (LEJ-uhnd)—someone who is among the best in what they do

variation (vair-ee-AY-shuhn)—a trick that is created by combining other tricks, one after the other

vert (VURT)—a style of BMX riding done on large U-shaped ramps called half-pipes

READ MORE

Mara, Wil. *Extreme BMX.* Sports on the Edge! New York: Marshall Cavendish Benchmark, 2012.

Mattern, Joanne. *BMX.* Action Sports. Vero Beach, Fla.: Rourke Pub., 2009.

McClellan, Ray. *BMX Freestyle.* Torque: Action Sports. Minneapolis: Bellwether Media, 2008.

INTERNET SITES

FactHound offers a safe, fun way to find Internet sites related to this book. All of the sites on FactHound have been researched by our staff.

Here's all you do:

Visit *www.facthound.com*

Type in this code: 9781429665018

Check out projects, games and lots more at
www.capstonekids.com

INDEX